Family-Friendly Web Sites for Kids

Family-Friendly Web Sites for Kids

by
Valerie L. Petro
and
Lauren E. Marley

Paulist Press
New York / Mahwah, N.J.

Book design by Lynn Else
Cover design by Valerie L. Petro

Library of Congress Cataloging-in-Publication Data

Petro, Valerie L. (Valerie Lea)
    Family-friendly web sites for kids / by Valerie L. Petro and Lauren E. Marley.
      p. cm.
    Includes glossary of terms.
    ISBN 0-8091-4020-9 (alk. paper)
    1. Christian children—Religious life—Computer network resources. 2. Christian education of children—Computer network resources. 3. Children's Web sites. I. Marley, Lauren E. (Lauren Elisabeth). II. Title.

BV1536.4.P48 2001
025.04—dc21

00-054854

Published by Paulist Press
997 Macarthur Boulevard
Mahwah, New Jersey 07430

www.paulistpress.com

Printed and bound in the
United States of America

To Mom and Dad

Contents

Acknowledgments viii

Getting Started 1

Ages 3 to 6 9

Ages 7 to 12 31

Ages 13 and Up 73

Glossary 113

Acknowledgments

I'd like to give thanks—

To my daughter Lauren, for providing inspiration and purpose for my life.

To Colonel Mark Johnson, for his integrity and faith (blind or otherwise).

To Carol, whose ethics and talent have always astounded me.

To all the students in my life, who have taught me to ask good questions.

To the gentle souls at Paulist Press, for their encouragement and grace.

Getting Started

Introduction

As a teacher, student, and Christian mother, I understand the attraction, as well as the danger, of allowing children access to the Internet. Surfing the web can inspire young minds, ignite creativity, and introduce tolerance of different cultures; it can just as easily result in fruitless hours of mindless searching.

As I explored the endless maze of educational and Christian-based web sites with my adolescent daughter, we discovered many sites failed to include the one essential ingredient necessary to engage the younger mind—namely—fun! While some sites include appropriate content and interesting graphics, the tone is often stuffy or patronizing. However, we did find some incredibly entertaining educational sites—rich in content and effective in presentation. Games, interactive online puzzles, and streaming audio can make for dynamic delivery of Christian-value-based education.

You will find the best of these sites listed, reviewed, and described in the pages that follow. The sites are categorized by age group. Some sites have been repeated, when appropriate, in multiple age groups. With each review providing icons that identify the site as having specific content—educational, religious content, and so forth, this book will quickly guide you (and your children) to suitable and relevant web sites. Additionally, I have rated each site based on fun/entertainment value, educational content, Christian content, ease of navigation, degree of commercialization, and overall safety.

A Little Technical Information

Many older browsers cannot take advantage of certain features in "state of the industry" web sites. In order to experience the many fun sites reviewed in these pages fully, you should have the most current version available.

The latest browser versions come preloaded with most of the plug-ins required for animation and music. If your browser does not have the appropriate plug-in, often the site you are visiting will have a link to a downloadable version.

You can stay up to date on the latest versions of the two most popular browsers, Netscape and Microsoft Internet Explorer by visiting their sites and downloading the latest upgrades.

Netscape: **http://www.netscape.com**

Internet Explorer: **http://www.microsoft.com/windows/ie/default.htm**

Net Privacy

The Federal Trade Commission wants you to know about the Child Online Privacy Act, enacted April 21, 2000, to protect children under the age of 13.

http://www.ftc.gov/ogc/coppa1.htm

http://www.ftc.gov/bcp/conline/pubs/online/kidsprivacy.pdf

The law prohibits any web site from collecting individually identifiable information from children under 13 without first obtaining parental consent or direct parental notification. This information may be used only to respond directly to the child's request and shall not be used to recontact the child for other purposes. The site may not distribute this information to third parties or give children under 13 the ability to post publicly individually identifiable contact information without prior parental consent. Additionally, a site may not entice a child under 13 to divulge more information than is needed to participate in an activity.

NOTE:
Most good sites make their privacy policy available and obvious and will usually post safety guidelines for children.

Software Aids

There are a number of good software applications and service providers that filter or limit access to inappropriate material and chat rooms or prevent the sending of personal information. The following sites are only a few samples of what is available. Please visit them to familiarize yourself with your options.

http://www.crayoncrawler.com/

http://www.yourownworld.com/index2.html

http://www.netnanny.com/

http://www.safesurf.com/

http://www.cyberpatrol.com/dyn_hm.htm

http://info.lifewayonline.com

While software and filters may limit the possibility of exposure to unwanted material, nothing replaces parental involvement. Please be aware of what sites your children visit, surf with them when you can, and be certain they understand that the Internet, like life, has rules that need to be followed.

Rules of the Road for Young Surfers

Get permission before you log on.

Never give out your real name, address, or phone number online.

Never agree to meet with anyone you've met online.

Don't use bad words or talk about inappropriate things.

Always remember that there is someone at the other end of your transmission who has feelings, just as you do. Be kind, and think before you type.

Don't try to scare or threaten anyone.

DON'T TYPE IN ALL CAPS—it's considered rude, the same as shouting, and it may get you thrown out of some chat rooms.

Don't send or post pictures of yourself.

Don't accept downloads from anyone you don't know in "real life" while online. This is one way computers get viruses.

Never open any unsolicited e-mail attachments.

Tell your parents if you receive e-mail addressed to you from someone you don't know.

Tell your parents if anything "weird" happens while you're online.

If you are new to forums or message boards (posted messages) and feel a bit awkward, it is all right to "lurk" for a while. Lurking means that you are observing, but not participating in, the discussion or activity.

If you are new to chat rooms, lurking is not good. It will make you seem unfriendly. When you go into a chat room, think of it as walking into a new classroom or a party. You would be expected to say hello to the group. Do not assume or expect that people will seek you out or entertain you. If you want to make friends, you must be friendly. Talk about your hobbies, interests, or your favorite music. If the chat room has a topic, talk about that.

Most of all, have fun and be yourself.

If you follow these few simple precautions, you will find that cyberspace is a wonderful place to play, learn, and discover.

Guide to the Icons

1. **Entertainment**—Movies, TV, sports, trivia, fads, and trends

2. **Activities**—Things to do online or off—crafts, projects, and games

3. **Educational**—School subjects, homework help, and reference materials

4. **Religious Content**—Biblical references, Bible study, Sunday School resources, and other religious content

5. **Story Time**—Reading, student writers, workshops, poetry, and articles

6. **Art and Music**—Visual arts, music instruction, and exhibits

7. **Discovery**—Space, culture, invention, nature, and applied sciences

8. **Caution**—Parents are encouraged to preview this site before allowing younger viewers to surf it alone

9. **Rating**—One to five starfish, five indicating the safest, most kid-friendly, noncommercial sites with no outside links.

Ages 3 to 6

All About Jesus

http://www.geocities.com/~perkinshome/children.html

Ages 3 to 12

Devotions

Bible Quiz

Coloring Pages

ABC Scavenger Hunt

Games and Puzzles, Jokes and Riddles

Online Reading

Bible Study: Numbered Bible lessons with several links to online Bibles

Aimed at two age groups—preschool to age 6, and 6 to 12—this site is well organized, entertaining, and educational. Its charming style and bright, simple graphics invite kids to participate. Lessons are numbered and easy to follow. This is an excellent resource for Bible study on the elementary level. Outside links present.

All God's Children

http://www.ilovejesus.com/allgodschildren/

Ages 3 to 10

Coloring Book Pages

Rainy Day Crafts

I Spy

Time for School

Word and Picture Puzzles

Drawing Lessons

Children's Prayers

Our Art Work

Just for Parents Link

Big, bright, and easy to navigate, this site is chockfull of Bible-themed activities to do online or off. Educational worksheets, games, and crafts with easy to follow directions for children under 10. Younger kids will enjoy the online version of "I Spy" and the printable coloring pages. Outside links and advertisements present.

Kidz Under Construction

http://home.at.net/~kidzunderconstruction/

Ages 3 to 6

Printable Coloring Pages

Fingerplays and Action Rhymes

Indoor Games

Songs

Recommended Links

Designed with Sunday School teachers in mind, this site offers instructions for acting out Bible verses with fun finger plays and rhymes, indoor games, and words to favorite Christian songs. Simple and straightforward, with easy navigation to all activities. Outside links. No advertisements.

Bible-Based Coloring Pages for Kids

http://www.christiananswers.net/kids/color%2Dbible.html

Ages 3 to 6

This page from the ChristianAnswers.net is a list of links to eighteen printable, full sized, coloring pages with themes taken from Genesis to Revelation. No advertisements. Outside links present.

Prayers

http://www.bedtime.com/html/prayers.html

Ages 3 and Up

Bedtime.com posts the words to Christian bedtime prayers, daily prayers, and before-dinner graces suitable for young children. Advertisements and outside links present.

Virtual Church Kids

http://www.virtualchurch.org/kids.htm

Ages 3 to 10

Coloring Pages

Clip Art

Stories

Virtual Tour

There are illustrated Bible stories, Bible coloring pages, and free Christian clip art to print out. Older kids can explore the different rooms of the Virtual Church at this extraordinary site filled with text, music, great outside links, and some amazing photos of churches and stained glass. Outside links, some to commercial sites.

Bry-Back Manor

http://www.cstone.net/~bry-back/index.html

Ages 3 to 6

Activity Pages

The Attic

Garden Fun

Holiday Fun

Recipes

Icon Extravaganza

Over 190 pages of printable activities! Coloring pages, mazes, word find, and more, designed for children with minimal or no reading skills. This site also features downloadable activities (Mac only) with lots of color and sound (holidays, colortime, dollhouse, and others), plus loads of free icons for your desktop. Advertisements and outside links present.

Chateau Meddybemps

http://www.meddybemps.com

Ages 3 to 6

Online Learning Activities
Just for Fun
Young Writers
Resources for Parents

Although this is a commercial site, Susan and Jerry Jindrich have dedicated most of it to early childhood development. Mix and match JavaScript games will amuse younger children who enter the cuckoo workshop. There is also an online interactive light show where visitors can light up a cat and mouse, tickle the moon, check out circus animals, and more.

Children's Storybooks Online

http://www.magickeys.com/books/

Ages 3 and Up

Online Stories

Coloring Pages

Riddles

Mazes

This site has illustrated stories to read online for three different age groups. For younger children with limited reading skills, there are animated counting stories. For older children, there are slightly longer stories with a moral. Be sure to check out the links to other literary sites. Outside links and advertisements present.

Coloring.com: Online Interactive Coloring Pages

http://www.coloring.com/

Ages 3 to 8

Online Coloring Pages

Contests

Gallery

This neat little site features pictures to color while online or print out and color off line. Choose your favorite theme among sports, holidays, animals, and more. Click the magic crayons to start coloring. You can choose textures and patterns too. If you become a member (e-mail address required) you can display your finished works in your own online gallery. Advertisements and outside links present.

FamilyFun.com: Crafts

http://www.familyfun.com/filters/mainindex/crafts.html

Ages 5 and Up

Let's Color	Wearable
Homemade Toys	Squish and Sculp
Recyclables	Homemade Gifts
From Nature	Holidays
Paper	Tips

This page from *FamilyFun* magazine has directions and diagrams for oodles of make-at-home crafts. Younger kids will require adult supervision, but some projects are simple enough for older kids to do by themselves. Advertisements, promotions, and outside links present.

Haring Kids

http://www.haringkids.com/

Ages 3 to 10

Activities

Art

Screen Saver

Coloring Book

Games

Lesson Plans

There is much to see at this deceptively simple site. Bright colors and Haring's unmistakable icons dance and morph while they speak of love and joy. There are Java picture puzzles and a downloadable application (PCs only) that lets you travel through a 3-D World while online. No advertisements or outside links.

Hop Pop Town

http://www.kids-space.org/HPT/index.html

Ages 3 to 6

Singing Leaves

Instruments Hall

Scenario Creator

Singing Stairs

Sing a Song

World Trip

You will need Shockwave and LiveAudio (download links present) to appreciate fully this compact musical site. Click and record online sounds to hear them played back in sequence, explore the scales, sing along with words and music, and hear music from around the world. No advertisements. Outside links present.

Kinderart: Art Education

http://www.kinderart.com/

Ages 3 and Up

Archives of Arts-and-Crafts Instructions and Diagrams
Library
Forum
Coloring Pages

Primarily designed by teachers, this site boasts a comprehensive archive of free arts-and-crafts "how to" instructions, with lesson plans covering architecture, crafts, drawing, printmaking, sculpture, textiles, and much more. Perfect foil for the rainy-day blues. Banner ads and other promotions present.

Kids Play Safe: Boowa and Kwala's HomePage

http://www.boowakwala.com/

Ages 3 to 10

Games
Online Coloring Pages
Musical Puzzles
Stories (and much more) in French or English

This wonderful site, which is updated regularly, is filled with curious graphics, self-directed animation, sounds, songs, and interactive learning games (for younger children). Mistletoe sings, clowns clap, and colors gurgle their name in the moving coloring book. If you become a member (requires an e-mail address only), the secret pages will be revealed to you. Younger kids will love this site. No advertisements or outside links.

Kids' Space: Show Your Art, Write Your ABCs, Share Your Music, and Make New Friends

---

http://www.kids-space.org/

Ages 3 to 8

Kids Art Gallery

StoryBook

Beanstalk

On Air Concert

World Wonder Map

Kids' Space mission statement proclaims it was created to foster literacy, artistic expression, and cross-cultural understanding among the world's children. At this site children from all over the world can share their ideas and traditions through personal web pages, posted messages, and "key pals." There is also a clickable World Wonder Map with links to outside web sites from different countries. No advertisements. Outside links present.

The Little Animals Activity Center

http://www.bbc.co.uk/education/laac/menu.html

Ages 3 to 10

Let's Make Something

A Numbers Game

Word Game

Music Game

Let's Read a Story

Simply designed pages for young to middle-school-age kids by the BBC. Printable directions for easy-to-make crafts, online interactive math games, word and music games (try Puzzlesnuff's Magicletters game), and an interactive storybook (Shockwave required). No advertisements. Links to the BBC host site.

PBS Kids

http://www.pbs.org/kids/

Ages 5 and Up

Arthur	Mister Rogers
Theodore Tugboat	Zoo
Barney	Noddy
Wimzie's House	Fun and Games
Dragon Tales	Teletubbies
Zoboomafoo	Babble On

All the PBS favorites are here. Read stories, print bookmarks and coloring pages, listen to music, or play online games. The site is quirky, however, as some activities of interest to younger surfers may be too complex or difficult for them to navigate alone. Overall a good, fun-filled site. No advertisements. Outside link to PBS Host site.

Peter Rabbit Home Page

---

http://www.peterrabbit.co.uk

Ages 5 and Up

Fun with Shapes

Pop-up Fun

Word Search

Peter's Picture Puzzle (requires Shockwave)

Print and Play

Dot to Dot

The full-screen Beatrix Potter illustrations are worth a visit to the "authorized and definitive" site about Peter Rabbit and Friends. Online readings and activities, printable Potter coloring pages, and e-postcards are all available for free. View video clips (QuickTime required) and sample learning games from the videos and CD ROMs for sale. This is a commercial site with no outside links.

The San Diego Zoo

http://www.sandiegozoo.com/

All Ages

Panda Cam

Wild Animal Park

CRES (Center for Reproduction of Endangered Species)

Postcards (beautiful animal pix to send as e-postcards or download)

Shopzoo.com

Wild Ideas

See gorillas, tropical aviaries, polar bears, chimps, tigers, and more! Watch the panda cam, download a movie, send a postcard, and read all about the fabulous animals at the San Diego Zoo. Fascinating and well designed, this site is filled with lush photos and solid information. The next best thing to being there. Plush toys are offered for sale at shopzoo.com. Outside links present.

StoryPlace: The Children's Digital Library

http://www.storyplace.org

Ages 3 to 6

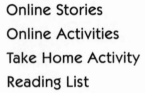

Online Stories

Online Activities

Take Home Activity

Reading List

Freda the Frog is your guide at this colorful site, updated regularly from the Public Library of Charlotte and Mecklenburg County. Freda reads online stories and narrates interactive games that teach preschoolers color, word, and number recognition. Available in English and Spanish. No advertisements. Outside links present.

Yak's Corner: America's Coolest Newsmagazine for Kids

http://www.yakscorner.com/

Ages 5 and Up

The Big Story

Animals

Yaktivities

Fun and Games

Your Art Gallery

Yak on the Road

The *Detroit Free Press* has done an excellent job creating a fun site aimed at what kids really care about—toys, games, fads, and food. The educational content is seasoned with big pictures and readable text in simple one-page formats, making it easy to navigate and fun to read. The home page carries a link to the grown-up version of the *Detroit Free Press*. Promotions, advertisements, and outside links present.

Ages 7 to 12

Haring Kids

http://www.haringkids.com/

Ages 3 to 10

Activities

Art

Screen Saver

Coloring Book

Games

Lesson Plans

There is much to see at this deceptively simple site. Bright colors and Haring's unmistakable icons dance and morph while they speak of love and joy. Java picture puzzles and a downloadable application (PCs only) that lets you travel through a 3-D World while online. No advertisements or outside links.

Leonardo's Workshop: An Art Adventure with Carmine Chameleon

http://www.sanford-artadventures.com/play/leonardo/

Ages 7 to 10

Create Art

Study Art

Student Gallery

Art Lessons

Newsletter

Travel back in time to visit da Vinci's workshop and learn about all the art materials available to the Renaissance artist. This site offers solid art instruction to the young artist with tips on technique, color, perspective, and proportion. Sponsored by Sanford Art Supplies. Advertisements, promotions, and outside links present.

Free Online Guitar Lessons: Tablature and Music Links

http://www.cyberfret.com/home.htm

Ages 8 and Up

Reading

Theory

Ear training

Chords and Arpeggios

Techniques, styles, and scales taught to you by a real guitar teacher and graduate of the Berklee College of Music. Log on, tune up, and get real with the blues, jazz, classical, or funk (requires RealPlayer). Outside links and advertisements present.

Piano on the Net

http://www.artdsm.com/music.html

Ages 8 and Up

Yes, it's true! You can learn how to play the piano on the Internet for free! This site begins with starter lesson number 1 and takes you through advanced studies in thirty-four lessons. Notes on composition and improvisation, with quizzes. You'll need QuickTime and a JavaScript-enabled browser and, of course, a keyboard. No advertisements. Outside links present.

Carnegie Museum of Natural History: Discovery Room Online

http://www.clpgh.org/cmnh/discovery/index.html

Ages 7 to 10

Meet the Beetles

Dinosaur Imposters

Dinosaur Jumble

Dinoscience

What's in a Name?

Get close enough to see the leg hairs on a bombardier beetle or test your skill at constructing a dinosaur. This page from the Carnegie Museum of Natural History entertains as it instructs young surfers. Links to the museum's home-page exhibit of Egyptian artifacts, where they reconstruct a face from a mummy. Advertisements and outside links present.

Planetpals Earthzone

http://www.planetpals.com/

Ages 7 to 10

Planet Earth and Ecology Facts

Recycling Tips

Crafts and Origami Patterns

Printable Coloring Pages

Green Links

Free recycling kit, e-mail stickers, printable coloring pages, card game, craft ideas, Kidz Club Planet pen pals, weather info, and Earth Day pages. Lots of earth-friendly activities here for younger kids—all designed to encourage them to think green. Advertisements and outside links present.

U.S. EPA Explorers Club

http://www.epa.gov/kids/

Ages 7 and Up

Air

Art Room

Science Room

Game Room

Plants and Animals

You and Your Environment

Although a bit hard to navigate, this site from the Environmental Protection Agency offers an interactive learning experience while teaching how to keep the environment clean and safe. Colorful illustrations report on the ozone layer, endangered species, air and water pollution, and what kids can do to help. No advertisements. Outside links present.

WonderKorner: The Question/Answer Place
for Curious Kids

http://www.peak.org/~bonwritr/wonder1.html

Ages 7 and Up

Wow! This is a great site! How do they put the lead in pencils? Why are sunsets so colorful? What did the ancient Romans eat? The site is an archive of questions posted by kids with links to web sites that supply the answers. Have a pressing query? You're allowed to ask *one* question (e-mail address requested). Free newsletter available. No advertisements. Outside links present.

White House for Kids

http://www.whitehouse.gov/WH/kids/html/kidshome.html

Ages 7 to 10

Map
History
Tour
White House Children
Pets in the White House
Presidents Past and Present
Newsletter

Here you can take a guided tour of the White House, see who lives and lived there, where it is, and who designed it. You can even send an e-mail to the president. There is also a newsletter available to download. No advertisements. Outside links present.

Crosswalk Sports

http://sports.crosswalk.com

Ages 10 and Up

Scoreboards

Stats

Features

Chat

Forums/Messages

More

NFL, NBA, NCAA—all the sports, scores, statistics, and news articles that you'd find at a first-rate news site, but Crosswalk.com reports the stories with an eye toward the Christian athlete. Quote of the Day, Athlete of the Week, *clean* jokes. Advertisements and outside links present.

FamilyFun.com: Crafts

http://www.familyfun.com/filters/mainindex/crafts.html

Ages 5 and Up

Let's Color

Homemade Toys

Recyclables

From Nature

Paper

Wearable

Squish and Sculp

Homemade Gifts

Holidays

This page from *FamilyFun* magazine has directions and diagrams for oodles of make-at-home crafts. Younger kids will require adult supervision, but some projects are simple enough for older kids to do by themselves. Advertisements, promotions, and outside links present.

Hall of Illusions: Interactive Optical Illusions

http://www.illusionworks.com/html/hall_of_illusions.html

Ages 7 and Up

Impossible Figures and Objects

Motion Illusion

Distortion Illusions

Camouflage Illusions

Motion After-effects

Auditory Illusion (Shockwave required)

Ever wonder how a barber pole works? Test your power of perception and learn the secrets of the impossible at the Hall of Illusions. Visual illusions are demonstrated, dissected, and explained. Unravel the mysteries of the impossible staircase, the scintillating grid, the Fraser Spiral, and other favorite optical mind benders. Shockwave and Java required (download link present). No advertisements. Outside links present.

Kinderart: Art Education

http://www.kinderart.com/

Ages 3 and Up

Archive of Arts-and-Crafts Instructions and diagrams

Library

Forum

Coloring Pages

Primarily designed by teachers, this site boasts a comprehensive archive of free arts-and-crafts "how to" instructions with lesson plans covering architecture, crafts, drawing, printmaking, sculpture, textiles, and much more. Perfect cure for the rainy-day blues. Banner ads and other promotions present.

KidsCom

http://www.kidscom.com

Ages 10 and Up

Around the World

Make New Friends

Kids Talk About

Just for Fun

Cool Stuff

This site stresses safety while giving kids a place to play. Excellent information on popular video game cheats, online Java- and Shockwave-based brain teasers, and two monitored chat rooms (separated by age group) active seven days a week—3 P.M. to 10 P.M. Central Time. A Loot Locker offers prizes to members (e-mail address required) from KidKash points earned online. Advertisements are clearly defined and age appropriate. Clearly defined outside link.

Kid's Domain Craft Exchange

http://www.kidsdomain.com/craft/index.html

Ages 7 and Up

Just for Fun

Make a Gift

Seasonal/Holiday Crafts

Recycled Projects

What's New

Other Crafty Sites

This page from Kid's Domain has a comprehensive list of crafts and indoor activities. Outside links may take you to some commercial sites. There are a lot of good ideas here, with links to pages that contain free downloadable games for both PCs and Macs. Advertisements and outside links present.

Kids OnLine

http://kids.singnet.com.sg/

Ages 7 and Up

Friendship Bracelets

Games (Shockwave required)

Lenny and Rasca Story archive

Toy Reviews

Sports

Who, How?

Pet Pages

Updated weekly, kids will want to bookmark this site from Singapore Net. There's lots of intelligent information on a variety of subjects from What is radioactivity? to Why are skunks smelly? Online games, stories, sports, projects with directions, illustrations, how-to diagrams, and more. Advertisements and outside links present.

Kids Play Safe: Boowa and Kwala's HomePage

http://www.boowakwala.com/

Ages 3 to 10

Games

Online Coloring Pages

Musical Puzzles

Stories (and much more) in French or English

This wonderful site, which is updated regularly, is filled with curious graphics, self-directed animation, sounds, songs, and interactive learning games (for younger children). Mistletoe sings, clowns clap, and colors gurgle their name in the moving coloring book. If you become a member (requires an e-mail address only), the secret pages will be revealed to you. Younger kids will love this site. No advertisements or outside links.

Kids' Space: Show Your Art, Write Your ABCs, Share Your Music, and Make New Friends

http://www.kids-space.org/

Ages 3 to 8

Kids Art Gallery
StoryBook
Beanstalk
On Air Concert
World Wonder Map

Kids' Space mission statement proclaims it was created to foster literacy, artistic expression, and cross-cultural understanding among the world's children. At this site, children all over the world can share their ideas and traditions through personal web pages, posted messages, and "key pals." There is also a clickable World Wonder Map with links to outside web sites from different countries. No advertisements. Outside links present.

Kids' Space Connection: An International Communication Site for Young Ambassadors

http://www.ks-connection.org/

Ages 8 to 12

Penpal Box
Bulletin Board
Web Kids Village
Go Outside!

This is the sister site to Kids' Space (www.kids-space.org) but with somewhat more advanced activities. Both sites offer a structured forum for children to share ideas electronically through personal web pages, posted messages, and "key pals." No advertisements. Outside links present.

Mann's Broccoli Town, USA: Kid's Club

http://www.broccoli.com/club/clubtoc.htm

Ages 7 to 12

Online Games

Coloring Book Pages

History of Broccoli

Health and Nutrition

Recipes

You wouldn't think a web site devoted to broccoli would be any fun—but here it is! There is more information here about broccoli than you ever thought possible, but the activities are an ingenious use of JavaScript—just try to work out the Tower of Hanoi and see what we mean. No advertisements. Outside links present.

Yak's Corner: America's Coolest Newsmagazine for Kids

http://www.yakscorner.com/

Ages 5 and Up

The Big Story

Kid News

Animals

Yaktivities

Fun and Games

Your Art

Yak on the Road

The *Detroit Free Press* has done an excellent job creating a fun site aimed at what kids really care about—toys, games, fads, and food. The educational content is seasoned with big pictures and readable text in simple one-page formats, making it easy to navigate and fun to read. The home page carries a link to the grown-up version of the *Detroit Free Press*. Promotions, advertisements, and outside links present.

Biography: The Web's Best Bios

http://www.biography.com/

Ages 7 and Up

Discussion
Classroom
On TV
Games

The home page highlights mostly movie and television personalities, but when we typed in *Churchill* we found fifteen matches, including a full page on the prime minister with links to related people and a list of his published works. This site, from A&E and the History Channel, is full of information, with short RealVideo BioByte clips (requires RealPlayer), study guides, message boards, and good outside links to history-related sites. Advertisements and outside links present.

Eyewitness Encyclopedia

http://eyewitness.dk.com/

Ages 7 and Up

History

Nature

Art

Geography

Science

Sports and Hobbies

Well designed and easy to navigate, this excellent site from Dorling Kindersley contains forty thousand pictures and two million words from the famous Eyewitness Encyclopedia series. Zoom in to read entire texts, complete with pictures, from any of these published works. Search by title, category, page number, or just browse through the library. This is a commercial site with promotions present. Requires Flash 5.0 from Macromedia, Inc. Outside links present.

Information Please Kids' Almanac

http://kids.infoplease.com/

Ages 7 and Up

All School Subjects
Current Events
Study Aids

A free reference site—online dictionary, encyclopedia, and homework help—just for kids, filled with facts about history, science, social studies, math, money, current events, and more. You'll also find tips on essay writing and study skills. Click on Homework Center and search for answers to specific questions on the Answer Page. Post your own question (e-mail address required) and the Homework Helpers will respond to homework questions not already posted. Advertisements and outside links present.

The Math Forum: Ask Dr. Math

http://www.mathforum.com/dr.math/

Ages 7 and Up

This page, hosted by Swarthmore College, is a list of links pointing to K–12 math questions with answers. Slim on design, straightforward answers are in text format only, although some contain links to outside sites that give more comprehensive answers. You can also submit your math question to Dr. Math (e-mail address required), but there is no guarantee of a reply. Outside links and advertisements present.

☆ ☆ ☆ ☆

MathStories.com: Math for Internet Generation

http://www.mathstories.com/

Ages 7 to 13

Keep young minds sharp during vacation breaks with over four thousand word problems available for printout. Very well organized, easy to navigate, and completely free (though a ten dollar donation is suggested), you'll find word problems for every level up to eighth grade. For the younger kids, there are math problems based on popular children's books and nursery rhymes. No advertisements or outside links.

Webmath

http://www.webmath.com/

Ages 6 and Up

General Math

Algebra

Graphs, Plots, and Geometric Stuff

Trigonometry

Calculus

More

Although commercial, this is the most practical, fully functional math site we've found—with an ingenious use of JavaScript. The animated version of simple addition is like having your own private math tutor on hand. We used the Webmath site to work out multiplying mixed fractions; not only did we get a correct answer, but we learned how to do it. Promotions, advertisements, and outside links present.

Amazon Interactive

http://www.eduweb.com/amazon.html

Ages 8 and Up

This page from Educational Web Adventures offers insight into the problems facing the Ecuadorian Amazon rain forest. Explore the dilemma of balancing survival, agriculture, and conservation through the eyes of the Quichua people. Try your hand at managing an ecotourism project with an online simulation. No advertisements. Outside links present.

The Children's Museum of Indianapolis

http://www.childrensmuseum.org/funonline/funonline.html

Ages 7 and Up

Kinetosaurs

Arts Workshop

CosmicQuest

Geo Mysteries

Water Clock Web Cam

Games

This page from the Children's Museum has activities for both online or off. Learn to make and move dinosaur sculptures; produce online theater with a story, music, and scenery you create; or just test your wits with an infuriating game of dots. Blast off with the Field Guide to the Universe, highlights of the night sky (updated monthly), an archive of spacecraft, and more. Java and Shockwave required. No advertisements. Outside links present.

Earth and Sky Radio Series

http://earthsky.com/Kids/

Ages 10 and Up

Archives of Earth and Sky Radio Series

Monthly Feature Articles

SkyWatching Forecast

Frequently Asked Science Questions

Star Guide

Science News Bulletin

The National Science Foundation sponsors this neat little site that archives Kathy's and Ed's nationally syndicated "Earth and Sky" radio spots. Listen online or browse feature articles archive for a variety of interesting earth and nature subjects. Online teachers' booklets, activities, and science news bulletins are also available. Don't forget to check on skywatching conditions! No advertisements. Outside links present.

The Exploratorium: The Museum of Science, Art, and Human Perception

http://www.exploratorium.edu/

Ages 8 and Up

From the famous hands-on science museum in San Francisco—live webcasts, featured exhibits, archives, incredible photos, activities, virtual tours, resources, illusions, observatory, and more. Regularly updated, the Exploratorium pages are packed with lots of stimulating and fun learning activities. Don't forget to test your reflexes against a fastball at the Science of Baseball page (requires Shockwave). Outside links present. Online store.

The Nine Planets: Just for Kids

http://www.tcsn.net/afiner/

Ages 7 to 10

Take a guided tour through our solar system. Hop aboard a spaceship and see planet surfaces up close. Notes offer facts, suggestions for sky watchers, and links for more in-depth exploration. Pictures from Mariner 10 and downloadable movies in QuickTime and MPG formats. No advertisements. Outside links present.

The San Diego Zoo

http://www.sandiegozoo.com/

All Ages

Panda Cam

Wild Animal Park

CRES (Center for Reproduction of Endangered Species)

Postcards (beautiful animal pix to send as e-postcards or download)

Shopzoo.com

Wild Ideas

See gorillas, tropical aviaries, polar bears, chimps, tigers, and more! Watch the panda cam, download a movie, send a postcard, and read all about the fabulous animals at the San Diego Zoo. Fascinating and well designed, this site is filled with lush photos and solid information. The next best thing to being there. Plush toys are offered for sale at shopzoo.com. Outside links present.

Aesop's Fables: Online Collection

http://www.pacificnet.net/~johnr/aesop/

Ages 7 and Up

Fables

Morals

Illustrations

This archive of over 655 children's fables is growing daily. Click on a title and read your choice of favorites from Aesop, the Brothers Grimm, Hans Christian Andersen, Ambrose Bierce, Jean de La Fontaine, L. Frank Baum, and Charles Dickens. A few of the fables have been recorded (requires RealAudio), so you can listen along as you read. Lesson plans with links to classroom resources. No advertisments. Outside links present.

Bean Town

---

http://www.calvary.com/beantown/

Ages 7 and Up

The Adventures of Willie and Grace

Bible Page—Stories and Puzzles

Cool Stuff 2 Do—Crafts, recipes, and science experiments

Factoids—Odd bits of information about bugs, animals, and planets

Willie and Grace are Christian kids who love to solve mysteries. Serial installments of mystery stories with a Christian message to read online with an archive of past episodes. A straightforward and simple design makes this site easy to navigate, interesting, and fun. Sponsored by Calvary Chapel, Monterey Bay, California. No advertisements. No outside links present.

Peter Rabbit Home Page

---

http://www.peterrabbit.co.uk

Ages 5 and Up

Fun with Shapes

Pop-Up Fun

Word Search

Peter's Picture Puzzle (requires Shockwave)

Print and Play

Dot to Dot

The full-screen Beatrix Potter illustrations are worth a visit to the "authorized and definitive" site about Peter Rabbit and Friends. Online readings and activities, printable coloring pages, and e-postcards are all available for free. View video clips (QuickTime required) and sample learning games from the videos and CD ROMs for sale. This is a commercial site with no outside links.

All About Jesus

http://www.geocities.com/~perkinshome/children.html

Ages 3 to 12

Devotions

Bible Quiz

Coloring Pages

ABC Scavenger Hunt

Games and Puzzles, Jokes and Riddles

Online Reading

Bible Study: Numbered Bible lessons with several links to online Bibles

Aimed at two age groups—preschool to age 6, and 6 to 12—this site is well organized, entertaining, and educational. Its charming style and bright, simple graphics invite kids to participate. Lessons are numbered and easy to follow. This is an excellent resource for Bible study on the elementary level. Outside links present.

Bible Study Tools

http://bible.crosswalk.com/

Ages 7 and Up

Well designed and easy to navigate, Bible Study Tools provides a premiere search engine for studying all parts of all translations of the Holy Bible, including the Latin Vulgate. Type in a keyword and corresponding Bible verses are displayed along with links to various commentaries, dictionaries, lexicons, notes, and sound clips (requires RealPlayer). Bible version preferences may be set so the site will remember them the next time you visit. This is an excellent resource. Advertisements and outside links present.

Kids Explorers: Adventures in the Rain Forest

http://www.ChristianAnswers.Net/kids/home.html

Ages 10 and Up

The Great Dinosaur Mystery

Video

Games

Scavenger Hunt

People (lifestyles of the people of the rain forest)

The great dinosaur mystery sets the stage with an educational excursion into how little we actually know about dinosaurs. Follow the trail and discover amber, fossils, and why the brontosaurus was a hoax. This site is full of color, sound, and good illustrations. Clickable RealAudio reading of God's story. Interspersed with Bible passages that reflect on God's work. No advertisements. Outside link to Christiananswer.net host site.

Kids' Mysteries

http://www.thecase.com/kids/

Ages 8 to 10

Chiller Mystery Stories

Quick-Solve

Magic Trick

Writing Contest

Mystery on TV

This is a small site with short mysteries to read and solve online. Young detectives are invited to complete a mystery story from a provided beginning. Good for younger audiences. Advertisements and outside links present.

The Jesus Film Project

---

http://www.jesusfilm.org/view/index.html

Ages 8 and Up

View the *Jesus Film* online in its entirety (requires RealPlayer) or listen to the full audio version (requires RealAudio). Promotions and outside links present.

A Worldwide Christmas Calendar

---

http://www.algonet.se/~bernadot/christmas/calendar.html

Ages 8 to 12

The page welcomes you with a drawing of a Christmas tree and 23 wrapped gifts. Click on a gift and it takes you to a page written by children, with drawings, stories, and descriptions of how Christmas day is spent in different countries. Very simple, sweet, and poignant. No advertisements. Outside links present.

Virtual Church: A Religious Experience Without Walls

http://www.virtualchurch.org/

Ages 7 and Up

Coloring Pages

Clip Art

Virtual Tour

Explore the rooms in the Virtual Church at this extraordinary site filled with text, music, great outside links, and some amazing photos of churches and stained glass. Lots of free Christian clip art and coloring pages to print out. No advertising. Outside links present.

Ages 13 and Up

Art Gallery of Angels

http://www.christusrex.org/www2/art/angels.html

Ages 12 and Up

If you like angels, you'll love this site! Click on a title, and your computer screen will be filled with some of the world's most famous images of divine grace. Promotions and outside links present.

The Vatican Museum

http://www.christusrex.org/www1/vaticano/0-Musei.html

Ages 12 and Up

A great collection of links to some of the world's finest art. Each link will take you to thumbnails of these masterpieces that can be clicked on for full-page window viewing. No advertisements. Outside links present.

Eyes on Art

http://www.kn.pacbell.com/wired/art2/index.html

Ages 11 and Up

ArtSpeak 101

Double Visions

No Fear o' Eras

Your True View

More

This is really a teacher's companion for art-education classes, presented by the Pacific Bell Knowledge Network, but it's a fun way to visit a superb collection of masterpieces and develop a visual vocabulary in the process. Online forms invite feedback to posted questions about color, line, symmetry, and other observable elements. There are outside links to online galleries (you may want to visit those before you let the younger ones surf alone).

☆☆☆☆

Renaissance Paintings: Famous Paintings in a Beautiful Format

http://www.christusrex.org/www2/art/

Ages 13 and Up

The title says it all! Here you will find some extraordinary examples of Renaissance painting. Click on the thumbnails for full-screen viewing of each masterpiece. Advertisements and outside links present.

Splendors of Christendom

http://www.christusrex.org/www1/splendors/splendors.html

Ages 13 and Up

A list of links to tours of some of the world's most beautiful Christian art and craftsmanship in churches, cathedrals, and monasteries. No advertisements. Outside links present.

The Whitney

http://whitney.artmuseum.net/

Ages 14 and Up

Current Exhibition
Personalized Tour
Time Line

A most sophisticated online exhibit of masterworks from the Whitney Museum. Parents may want to preview this site or use the *My Tour* feature, which allows a customized version of the current exhibition. Once past the elaborate navigation, a time line guides you through decade after decade of incredible art and also points of historical context. No advertisements. Outside links present.

ChristianTeens.Net

http://www.christianteens.net/main.shtml

Ages 13 and Up

Christian Music

WebTools

Christian Life

Education Resources

Games

Chat

Forums

This site is loaded with fun, information, and great links. Christian music reviews, MIDIs, video clips, web-master tools, downloads, online games, chat, forums, school and college prep information, and lots of pages devoted to Christian life and more. No advertisements. Outside links present.

Free Online Guitar Lessons: Tablature and Music Links

http://www.cyberfret.com/home.htm

Ages 8 and Up

Reading

Theory

Ear Training

Chords and Arpeggios

Techniques, styles, and scales taught to you by a real guitar teacher and graduate of the Berklee College of Music. Log on, tune up, and get real with the blues, jazz, classical, or funk (requires RealPlayer). Outside links and advertisements present.

☆☆☆☆

Piano on the Net

---

http://www.artdsm.com/music.html

Ages 8 and Up

Yes, it's true! You can learn how to play the piano on the Internet for free! This site begins with starter lesson number 1 and takes you through advanced studies in thirty-four lessons. Notes on composition and improvisation, with quizzes. You'll need QuickTime and a JavaScript-enabled browser and, of course, a keyboard. No advertisements. Outside links present.

The UrbanCross Network

---

http://www.urbancross.com/

Ages 14 and Up

Keep up to date on Christian hip-hop gospel music. Read news and reviews about independent Christian music makers, listen to audio clips, vote on the GospelForce Top 7, or just shop the music store. Advertisements and outside links present.

Academy of Achievement

http://www.achievement.org/

Ages 11 and Up

Gallery of Achievers

Achievement TV

Achiever's Club

Library

Steps to Success

A very inspirational site, good for anyone interested in developing his or her personal best. The Gallery includes top "movers and shakers" in the fields of art, business, public service, science and exploration, and sports. Read profiles, biographies, interviews, and quotations from some of the leading minds of the last hundred years. Promotions and outside links present.

Africam Virtual Game Reserve

http://www.africam.com/

Ages 12 and Up

Leopard Cam	Message Boards
Eagle Cam	Ask the Experts
Animal Guide	Bird Field Guide
Chat	Picture of the Month Competition
Conservation	African Arts

View wildlife in its natural habitat live from South Africa. Pick camera views from Sabi Sabi, Djuma Game Reserve, Kruger National Park, or just let Cam Scan guide you through a virtual tour of South Africa's wilderness. Enter the Picture of the Day contest, post your observations on the message board, ask a question in the Expert's Forum, or discuss conservation issues in the chat room. The field guides are brilliant. This site is as exciting as it is real. Advertisements and outside links present.

American Memory: American Memory from the Library of Congress

http://lcweb2.loc.gov/

Ages 10 and Up

Collection Finder

Learning Page

Search

Search this incredible site maintained by the Library of Congress by keyword, author, or title on all subjects American. The entire text may not be posted, but you will find a gold mine of facts and information, maps, drawings, picture files, and video clips. Start at the Features index to get a taste of what is available. No advertisements. Outside links present.

Data Services

---

http://aa.usno.navy.mil/AA/AAmap.html

Ages 10 and Up

Hosted by the U.S. Naval Observatory, this page is a list of links for astronomical applications. Check out data on recent and upcoming eclipses of the sun and moon, equinoxes, solstices, and the dates of Ash Wednesday and Easter. No advertisements. Outside links present.

A Global View from Space

---

http://sdcd.gsfc.nasa.gov/ISTO/dro/global/page1.html

Ages 12 and Up

Another outstanding page from NASA offering satellite views of the Earth. Although it's a bit slow to load, the images are phenomenal and worth the wait. We were able to track a storm moving across our state by zooming in on the world map and clicking Cloud Cover. No advertisements. Outside links present.

Galileo Project Home Page

http://www.jpl.nasa.gov/galileo/

Ages 12 and Up

The spacecraft Galileo has been studying the Jupiter system since 1995, and NASA has devoted this page to bringing home the latest information, images, news archives, and all spacecraft activities. Excellent educational resources are here, as well as instructions on building a scale model of the Galileo spacecraft. This site is easy to navigate, well designed, and filled with stunning photographs. No advertisements. Outside links present.

Greatest Engineering Achievements of the Twentieth Century

http://www.greatachievements.org/

Ages 10 and Up

Airplane	Internet
Automobile	Television
Electrification	Spacecraft
Computers	Telephone
Radio	More

This compact site explains the history, with a time line, of the greatest achievements of the twentieth century. Printable version available for downloading. Brought to you by the National Academy of Engineering. No advertisements or outside links.

How Things Work: The Physics of Everyday Life

http://rabi.phys.virginia.edu/HTW/

Ages 12 and Up

This site, hosted by the University of Virginia, answers hundreds of physics questions posted by students and others. Professor of physics Louis A. Bloomfield offers in-depth explanations of how everyday things—such as air conditioners, roller coasters, thermometers, and water faucets—do what they do. If you search by keyword, topic, and date of posting and still can't find your answer, a form is available to e-mail Dr. Bloomfield a question. Outside links and book promotion present.

Virtual Reality Moon Phase Pictures

http://tycho.usno.navy.mil/vphase.html

Ages 10 and Up

Have an overwhelming urge to howl? Check the current phase of the moon at this site hosted by the U.S. Naval Observatory. You can also check the phase of the moon for any date and time between 1800 and 2199. Click on the link to the home page and you will be able to set your atomic clock. No advertisements. Outside links present.

The Invention Dimension

http://web.mit.edu/afs/athena.mit.edu/org/i/invent/

Ages 12 and Up

Inventor's Archive
Awards Program Info
Inventor's Handbook

Find out who invented the Slinky, the skateboard, the microchip, and more at this MIT-hosted site. Learn what intellectual property is and how to apply for a patent in the online Inventor's Handbook. No advertisements. Outside links present.

The Religious Movements Homepage @ The University of Virginia

http://religiousmovements.lib.virginia.edu

Ages 12 and Up

Well designed and easy to navigate, this site from the University of Virginia alphabetically lists hundreds of religions old and new. Here you will find comprehensive group profiles that explore the history, sacred texts, and beliefs from Anabaptists and the birth of the Amish, to the more controversial Heaven's Gate, complete with outside links to other in-depth resources. This site may not be suitable for all viewers, so please surf with caution. No advertisements. Outside links present.

U.S. EPA Explorers Club

http://www.epa.gov/kids/

Ages 7 and Up

Air
Art Room
Science Room
Game Room
Plants and Animals
You and Your Environment

Although a bit hard to navigate, this site from the Environmental Protection Agency offers an interactive learning experience while teaching how to keep the environment clean and safe. Colorful illustrations report on the ozone layer, endangered species, air and water pollution, and what kids can do to help. No advertisements. Outside links present.

WonderKorner: The Question/Answer Place for Curious Kids

http://www.peak.org/~bonwritr/wonder1.htm

Ages 7 and Up

Wow! This is a great site! How do they put the lead in pencils? Why are sunsets so colorful? What did the ancient Romans eat? The site is an archive of questions posted by kids with links to web sites that supply the answers. Have a pressing query? You're allowed to ask *one* question (e-mail address requested). Free newsletter available. No advertisements. Outside links present.

FreeZone: Where Kids Connect for Safe, Interactive Fun Online

http://www.freezone.com/

Ages 8 to 15

Monitored Chat Rooms	Schoolwork Help
Special Guest Chats	Sports
Bulletin Boards	Pop Culture
WebTools	Newsletter
Advice	Online Games

More than a safe site, this is truly a kids' community. Well monitored and easy to navigate, with lots of news, interactivity, and discussion on sports, school, culture, and relationships, these pages are written almost entirely by its young members. The chat rooms fill quickly, and you must become a member to join in (e-mail address required). The advertisements are appropriate and clearly marked as ads. Outside links present.

Girl's World: A Girl's World Online—
Where Girls and Teens Rule the Web

http://www.agirlsworld.com

Ages 12 to 16

Advice	Features	Surveys
Diaries	Chat	Pen Pals
Entertainment	Contests	Mall

A Girl's World Online Club describes itself as the only free online magazine written entirely by girls and teens. There's plenty to see here and lots of advice about dating, boys, family issues, and schoolwork. Nonmembers can read feature articles on celebrities, music, sports, pets, and advice on more serious issues. For a five-dollar fee (or a posted article) and a parent's signature, girls can enter hosted chat rooms, play games, download graphics, or take an online class in babysitting. Good content. Advertisements and outside links present.

KidsCom

---

http://www.kidscom.com

Ages 10 and Up

Around the World

Make New Friends

Kids Talk About

Just for Fun

Cool Stuff

This site stresses safety while giving kids a place to play. Excellent information on popular video game cheats, online Java- and Shockwave-based brain teasers, and two monitored chat rooms (separated by age group) active seven days a week—3 P.M. to 10 P.M. Central Time. A Loot Locker offers prizes to members (e-mail address required) from KidKash points earned online. Advertisements are clearly defined and age appropriate. Clearly defined outside link.

Kid's Domain Craft Exchange

http://www.kidsdomain.com/craft/index.html

Ages 7 and Up

Just for Fun

Make a Gift

Seasonal/Holiday Crafts

Recycled Projects

What's New

Other Crafty Sites

This page from Kid's Domain has a comprehensive list of crafts and indoor activities. Outside links may take you to some commercial sites. There are a lot of good ideas here, with links to pages that contain free downloadable games for both PCs and Macs. Advertisements and outside links present.

Biography: The Web's Best Bios

http://www.biography.com/

Ages 7 and Up

Search Engine   Magazine

Discussion   On TV

Classroom   Games

The home page highlights mostly movie and television personalities, but when we typed in *Churchill* we found fifteen matches, including a full page on the prime minister with links to related people, and a list of his published works. This site, from A&E and the History Channel, is full of information, with short RealVideo BioByte clips (requires RealPlayer), study guides, message boards, and good outside links to history-related sites. Advertisements and outside links present.

Calculators on Line

http://www-sci.lib.uci.edu/HSG/RefCalculators.html

Ages 13 and Up

There is a link to any kind of calculator you can think of here—mathematical, statistical, science, astrophysics, engineering, physics. This is the place for atmosphere/weather unit conversions, Old English measurement, exponential expression, golf handicap, weight and balance, fractal chaos, seesaws, Mayan calendar, knitting patterns—and the list goes on and on. No advertisements. Outside links present. ⭐⭐⭐⭐

The Math Forum: Ask Dr. Math

http://www.mathforum.com/dr.math/

Ages 7 and Up

This page, hosted by Swarthmore College, is a list of links pointing to K–12 math questions with answers. Slim on design, straightforward answers are in text format only, although some contain links to outside sites that give more comprehensive answers. You can also submit your math question to Dr. Math (e-mail address required), but there is no guarantee of a reply. Outside links and advertisements present. ⭐⭐⭐⭐

Eyewitness Encyclopedia

http://eyewitness.dk.com/

Ages 7 and Up

History

Nature

Art

Geography

Science

Sports and Hobbies

Well designed and easy to navigate, this excellent site from Dorling Kindersley contains forty thousand pictures and two million words from the famous Eyewitness Encyclopedia series. Zoom in to read entire texts, complete with pictures, from any of these published works. Search by title, category, page number, or just browse through the library. This is a commercial site with promotions present. Requires Flash 5.0 from Macromedia, Inc. Outside links present.

Information Please Kids' Almanac:
Online Dictionary, Encyclopedia, and Homework Help

http://kids.infoplease.com/

Ages 7 and Up

All School Subjects
Current Events
Study Aids

A free reference site—online dictionary, encyclopedia, and homework help—just for kids, filled with facts about history, science, social studies, math, money, current events, and more. You'll also find tips on essay writing and study skills. Click on Homework Center and search for answers to specific questions on the Answer Page. Post your own question (e-mail address required) and the Homework Helpers will respond to homework questions not already posted. Advertisements and outside links present.

Map Collection Home Page—
From the Library of Congress

---

http://memory.loc.gov/ammem/gmdhtml/gmdhome.html

Ages 12 and Up

Another incredible web page from the Library of Congress: Map Collections 1544–1999. Here you can download or zoom in and view online maps of state parks, military battles, transportation and communication routes, exploration, and more. Search by keyword, subject, location, or title. Excellent homework resource. No advertisements. Outside links present.

☆☆☆☆

Martindale's "The Reference Desk"

---

http://www-sci.lib.uci.edu/HSG/Ref.html#fast

Ages 12 and Up

This is a fabulous site composed of links to all sorts of online reference resources: dictionaries, maps, language translation, patents and trademark, science and health, courses in HTML/Java, freeware, construction, environment and safety, gardening, and more. Bookmark this one! No advertisements. Outside links present.

Webmath

http://www.webmath.com/

Ages 6 and Up

General Math

Algebra

Graphs, Plots, and Geometric Stuff

Trigonometry

Calculus

More

Although commercial, this is the most practical, fully functional math site we've found—with an ingenious use of JavaScript. The animated version of simple addition is like having your own private math tutor on hand. We used the Webmath site to work out multiplying mixed fractions; not only did we get a correct answer, but we learned how to do it. Promotions, advertisements, and outside links present.

Wordsmyth

http://www.wordsmyth.net/home.shtml

Ages 13 and Up

This site goes far beyond an ordinary online dictionary. Here you can find words when you know the definitions, or use the anagram or word-jumble solver. Create a word quiz or glossary and download it as a PDF file (great study aid). Post to the word forum, subscribe to Words of the Week or the Wordsmyth Watch Newsletter (e-mail address required). Wordsmyth also offers free access tools, such as a floating remote window and a lookup button for your browser. No advertisements. Outside links present.

Amazon Interactive

http://www.eduweb.com/amazon.html

Ages 8 and Up

This page from Educational Web Adventures offers insight into the problems facing the Ecuadorian Amazon rain forest. Explore the dilemma of balancing survival, agriculture, and conservation through the eyes of the Quichua people. Try your hand at managing an ecotourism project with an online simulation. No advertisements. Outside links present.

The Children's Museum of Indianapolis

http://www.childrensmuseum.org/funonline/funonline.html

Ages 7 and Up

Kinetosaurs

Arts Workshop

CosmicQuest

Geo Mysteries

Water Clock Web Cam

Games

This page from the Children's Museum has activities for both online or off. Learn to make and move dinosaur sculptures; produce online theater with a story, music, and scenery you create; or just test your wits with an infuriating game of dots. Blast off with the Field Guide to the Universe, highlights of the night sky (updated monthly), an archive of spacecraft, and more. Java and Shockwave required. No advertisements. Outside links present.

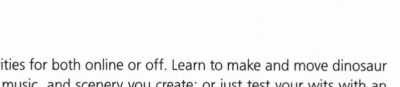

Earth and Sky Radio Series

http://earthsky.com/Kids/

Ages 10 and Up

Archives of Earth and Sky Radio Series

Monthly Feature Articles

SkyWatching Forecast

Frequently Asked Science Questions

Star Guide

Science News Bulletin

The National Science Foundation sponsors this neat little site that archives Kathy's and Ed's nationally syndicated "Earth and Sky" radio spots. Listen online or browse feature articles archive for a variety of interesting earth and nature subjects. Online teachers' booklets, activities, and science news bulletins are also available. Don't forget to check on skywatching conditions! No advertisements. Outside links present.

Envirolink Home Page

http://www.envirolink.org/

Ages 13 and Up

Projects
Library
EnviroLink News Service
Features
Youth Environment Community

This is just the site for teens who think green. Lots of links and resources to inspire responsible thought (and action) toward the environment. Well designed and easy to navigate. Advertisements and outside links present.

The Exploratorium: The Museum of Science, Art, and Human Perception

http://www.exploratorium.edu/

Ages 8 and Up

From the famous hands-on science museum in San Francisco—live webcasts, featured exhibits, archives, incredible photos, activities, virtual tours, resources, illusions, observatory, and more. Regularly updated, the Exploratorium pages are packed with lots of stimulating and fun learning activities. Don't forget to test your reflexes against a fastball at the Science of Baseball page (requires Shockwave). Outside links present. Online store.

The San Diego Zoo

http://www.sandiegozoo.com/

All Ages

Panda Cam

Wild Animal Park

CRES (Center for Reproduction of Endangered Species)

Postcards (beautiful animal pix to send as e-postcards or download)

Shopzoo.com

Wild Ideas

See gorillas, tropical aviaries, polar bears, chimps, tigers, and more! Watch the panda cam, download a movie, send a postcard, and read all about the fabulous animals at the San Diego Zoo. Fascinating and well designed, this site is filled with lush photos and solid information. The next best thing to being there. Plush toys are offered for sale at shopzoo.com. Outside links present.

Bible Study Tools

http://bible.crosswalk.com/

Ages 7 and Up

Well designed and easy to navigate, Bible Study Tools provides a premiere search engine for studying all parts of all translations of the Holy Bible, including the Latin Vulgate. Type in a keyword and corresponding Bible verses are displayed along with links to various commentaries, dictionaries, lexicons, notes, and sound clips (requires RealPlayer). Bible version preferences may be set so the site will remember them the next time you visit. This is an excellent resource. Advertisements and outside links present. ☆☆☆☆

The Jesus Film Project

http://www.jesusfilm.org/view/index.html

Ages 8 and Up

View the *Jesus Film* online in its entirety (requires RealPlayer) or listen to the full audio version (requires RealAudio). Promotions and outside links present. ☆☆☆☆

Kids Explorers: Adventures in the Rain Forest

http://www.ChristianAnswers.Net/kids/home.html

Ages 10 and Up

The Great Dinosaur Mystery

Video

Games

Scavenger Hunt

People (lifestyles of the people of the rain forest)

The great dinosaur mystery sets the stage with an educational excursion into how little we actually know about dinosaurs. Follow the trail and discover amber, fossils, and why the brontosaurus was a hoax. This site is full of color, sound, and good illustrations. Clickable RealAudio reading of God's story. Interspersed with Bible passages that reflect on God's work. No advertisements. Outside link to Christiananswer.net host site.

Live Western Wall Camera at Aish

http://aish.com/wallcam/

Ages 12 and Up

Devoted to advice and meditations on the Jewish faith, this astounding site also offers insight into our Christian roots. Here you can view a live cam of the Western Wall of the Temple Mount in Jerusalem and learn the Wall's incredible history. There is also a RealAudio tour of the adjacent labyrinth of tunnels and passageways revealed to the world in 1996. Advertisements and outside links present.

On Demand Vatican Radio

http://www.vaticanradio.org/
http://www.wrn.org/ondemand/vatican.html

Ages 13 and Up

Listen to Vatican Radio online. Fifteen minute archived clips, updated daily (requires RealPlayer). No advertisements. Outside links present.

Teen Advice OnLine

http://www.teenadviceonline.org/

Ages 13 and Up

Dating, depression, drugs, violence, sex, morality, peer pressure—these are but a few of the issues facing teens today. This site offers nonprofessional advice from peers in the form of posted and archived suggestions to a host of problems. Teen Advice Online claims no religious affiliation and may not be appropriate for all teens. However, sometimes the best medicine is simply to be heard. Articles, forum, monitored chat, and an extensive list of emergency hot-line phone numbers to call. No advertisements. Promotions and outside links present.

☆☆☆☆

The Way of the Cross

http://www.christusrex.org/www1/jvc/index.html

Ages 13 and Up

This is a devotional exercise that follows the geographical and physical layout of the painful path taken by Jesus to Calvary. Pictures accompany prayers and devotional text from the Last Supper and the Garden of Gethsemane to the Resurrection. A thought-provoking site that provides an emotional walk with Christ through the fifteen Stations of the Cross. No advertisements. Outside links present.

Youthwalk Online

http://www.youthwalk.org/

Ages 13 and Up

Intelligently written in an upbeat style for Christian teens, this is a well-designed e-version of *Youthwalk* magazine, with feature articles, columns, music reviews, reflections, and more. There is also the Cafe YouthTalk forum, where teens can respond to posted questions. Promotions and outside links present.

Glossary

Adobe Acrobat File. *See* PDF.

Banner Ad—An image advertising a commercial product or service. Clicking on a banner ad usually takes you to the advertiser's web site.

Bookmark—A feature of most web browsers that enables you to file the URL (or address) of a web page that you will want to revisit. Bookmarks can be saved by categories or organized so you can use them easily. To use, you click on the bookmark rather than retyping the URL.

Browser—Software, like Netscape and Internet Explorer, that enables you to access and display various kinds of Internet resources, usually web page documents.

Cam—A digital camera that feeds images to an Internet site, enabling you to view live action of people, places, or things. Some web cams take single pictures, which are updated periodically; others provide streamed (ongoing) video images.

CD ROM—Compact Disk (Read Only Memory) optical data storage medium using the same physical format as audio compact discs, readable by a computer with a CD-ROM drive.

Chat Room—A channel or web page where real time (simultaneous) communication with multiple persons is possible.

Client—Software that resides on a user's computer and can contact a server to communicate in a specific manner; for example, web-browser clients, e-mail clients, and so forth.

Clip art—Typically, a simple black and white graphic image inserted into text documents, used to indicate a theme.

Cookie—A piece of information stored in a user's browser (at the request of a web server) that can be retrieved by the initial server or other web servers at later times. The information stored in the cookie may record a user's preferences about how a site is viewed, track the user's habits in visiting that or related sites, or save other small amounts of information that a site wants to track about a user. Browsers often can be configured to allow or disallow cookies under specific conditions, but by default on most browsers a user is unaware when a cookie is sent or retrieved.

Cyberspace—Coined by William Gibson in his novel *Neuromancer* (Ace Books, 1984). Colloquially refers to the feeling of space, place, or landscape in the imagination, experienced while online.

Database—A collection of data electronically organized and stored in a way that makes it easy to sort, select, and retrieve.

Download—To move a file from another computer to your computer, often by requesting it at a web site. The opposite action is to upload, or transfer, a copy of a file from your computer to another one.

Emoticon—A combination of keyboard characters that form a facial expression. To see an emoticon, tip your head toward your left shoulder. The most widely used emoticon is :-) the "smiley."

E-postcard—A virtual postcard sent though e-mail. It usually contains images, text, and sound.

FAQ (Frequently Asked Questions)—A list of the most common questions on a particular subject, with answers. Very helpful when you are trying to install or use new software, for example.

Flash—(Or "Shockwave Flash") A file format for delivering interactive vector graphics and animation on the World Wide Web, developed by Macromedia.

Home Page—The main or first page on a web site.

Host—A computer that acts as a server, processing user requests for various information.

HTML (Hypertext Markup Language)—The language or codes used to create documents that can be viewed with your web-browser. HTML codes determine how a piece of text or a graphic or other element will appear on your screen.

Icon—A small picture representing a labeled button. When an icon is clicked, some action is performed such as opening a web page or downloading a file.

Interactive—A web site that allows you to respond while online. This type of programming is typical of games and ordering online, for example.

ISP (Internet Service Provider)—A company that provides customers with access to the Internet, e-mail addresses, and often space for a personal web page.

Keyword—A word, or small set of words, designed to convey the subject or topic of a document.

Link (or Hyperlink)—Clickable connections to other web pages. Links are usually identified by colored, underlined text describing the destination.

LiveAudio—Software that supports transmissions of real-time, streamed audio.

Login—Account name or user ID and password used to gain access to a computer-based service provided by a network or other remote system.

Mailing List—A computerized system used to distribute e-mail or posts from one person to many other people in the group who are on the list.

Message Board—Messages posted on a web site by members of a particular interest group, club, or organization. Message boards are available for a wide variety of topics.

MIDI (Musical Instrument Digital Interface, pronounced Middy)—A popular file format that allows digital transference of high quality audio over the Internet.

Morph—The animated transformation of one image into another by gradually distorting and moving certain points of the first image until they correspond and mutate into a second image.

MPG (Moving Picture Experts Group)—A compression format developed for efficient storage and transmission of video and movie data.

Netiquette—Code of behavior, or etiquette, used on the Internet.

Online—Usually refers to being connected to the Internet.

Online Store—A commercial web site used for direct sales of commercial products or services.

Password—A combination of characters (usually letters and numbers) used to verify the identity of a user when logging onto a system or site.

PDF (Portable Document Format)—A file format that allows a document to be displayed in its original format regardless of the application in which it originally was created.

Plug-In—Task-oriented software that works in conjunction with a browser to expand its capabilities, for example, the Shockwave plug-in, which allows dynamic web-page content presentation.

QuickTime—One of several software programs available to play synchronized graphics, sound, video, and music.

RealAudio—A specific brand of streaming audio.

RealPlayer—One of several software programs available to play synchronized graphics, sound, video, and music.

Real-time—Most commonly used to describe an application that provides text or video received within seconds of transmission.

RealVideo—Software tool that supports transmissions of real-time, live, or prerecorded video.

115

Search Engine—Web-based software that allows you to query a database by inputting keywords; it returns web pages that match your queries.

Server—A computer dedicated to providing a specific service that allows computers connected to the Internet to communicate with each other.

Service Provider. *See* ISP.

Shockwave Player—A browser plug-in that allows you to view interactive multimedia web contents including games, animation, and entertainment.

Spam—Inappropriate postings, or unsolicited, usually commercial, e-mail.

Streaming Audio—Software tool that supports transmissions of real-time, live, or prerecorded audio.

Surf, surfing—Used by analogy to describe a sense of skimming over (waves of) information while traveling around the web.

Thumbnail—From thumbnail sketch. On a web page, a thumbnail is a small picture linked to a larger version of itself. Thumbnails are used to lessen the download time

of web pages containing many images that may require close examination, such as art portfolios.

Trojan Horse—A program that seems to be harmless but starts harmful functions after it has been installed.

URL (Uniform Resource Locator)—The standard way to give the address of any resource, usually a web site, on the Internet. An example is http://www.paulistpress.com.

Virtual—The sense of reality created by interacting in a digital environment.

Virus—A piece of software that surreptitiously inserts or appends itself to legitimate programs or data files so that it can spread to even more programs or data files on the same computer. Viruses often damage or destroy files on the "infected" system.

Webmaster—The person in charge of a web server and, in some cases, responsible for its content.

Worm—A program whose sole purpose is to propagate itself across networks to other computers and other users without any cooperation from the victims. Worms often slow down computers, networks, and users deluged by the traffic. Worms are often one kind of Trojan Horse.